It's
Actually a
GOOD
Thing

It's
Actually a
GOOD
Thing

J.L. WITTERICK

ARCHWAY
PUBLISHING

Archway Publishing books may be ordered through booksellers or by contacting:

Archway Publishing
1663 Liberty Drive
Bloomington, IN 47403
www.archwaypublishing.com
1-(888)-242-5904

Because of the dynamic nature of the Internet, any web addresses or links contained in this book may have changed since publication and may no longer be valid. The views expressed in this work are solely those of the author and do not necessarily reflect the views of the publisher, and the publisher hereby disclaims any responsibility for them.

Illustrator and Photographer: Philip Estrada

Certain stock imagery © Thinkstock.
Any people depicted in stock imagery provided by Thinkstock are models, and such images are being used for illustrative purposes only.

ISBN: 978-1-4808-1184-3 (e)
ISBN: 978-1-4808-1183-6 (sc)

Printed in the United States of America.

Archway Publishing rev. date: 10/06/2014

With deep gratitude to Tony Robbins and Oprah Winfrey,
who helped me understand that our focus is our reality.

Introduction

I graduate second in my class in high school, finance my education from academic scholarships, maintain an A average in a top business school, work for one of the most brilliant investors of all time, and then start an investment firm which delivers superior investment performance over the long term. Along the way, I also write an international bestselling novel.

In my life up to now, I don't know anything but success layered upon success. So when my largest client leaves and we wind down the business that I founded, people ask me, are you okay?

They are surprised when I say to them, "It's actually a good thing."

Truth is, I am just as surprised that I would say this, because I have been driven all my life, and now there are no lines on the road. If I can think this way about what just happened to me, maybe there are other things that I can think in this way about as well.

All of us have setbacks of one kind or another, right? No one goes through life without a few wounds. Healing is easy for some, but for others, not so much.

I want to share with you some of the unexpected positives that can come from having "bad stuff" happen to you ... because they exist.

If I can make you smile and think a little differently, well then maybe what happened to me was actually a good thing!

J.L Witterick

"la, la, la"

Plain-Looking?

It's Actually a GOOD Thing

People love you for your personality, and you don't worry about losing your good looks.

Developing a pleasing personality is something you can control. Being born with naturally good looks is not. Time is a great equalizer. By adapting healthy eating habits and exercise, you can improve your appearance on a relative basis, because aging takes its toll on everyone including those who are born naturally good-looking.

Doing badly, really badly?

It's Actually a GOOD Thing

Helps you understand people down on their luck, who you thought were just lazy before.

During the financial crisis, I am as close to being broken as anyone can be without actually being broken. My company manages money for pension funds, and I feel a personal responsibility for all those retired people. So when the stock market plummets and we lose money for our clients, it feels like someone punches me in the stomach hard. We literally work night and day, coming up with strategies to make the money back. Thankfully, we make all the money back and more, but that experience changes me. I understand for the first time in my life that it is possible to be in a place so dark that you cannot find the light, even on the brightest day. It makes me truly understand how it feels to do badly, really badly, and I think I am more compassionate because of what happened.

Can't buy your girlfriend
a real diamond ring?

It's Actually a GOOD Thing

It's better that the rock
is fake than the love.

What's real is real, and a diamond in the end is just
a very hard rock.

Don't have a trust fund?

It's Actually a GOOD Thing

You won't become lazy just sitting around waiting for those monthly cheques.

When you grow up with nothing, you want to give your kids everything. You don't realize that by doing so, you're not really helping them. I say this honestly because it is something that I struggle with. A good friend of mine manages money for high-net-worth families, and she tells me that the kids who are given large amounts of money lose their motivation and initiative and are not happier. The inherited wealth deprives them of the satisfaction of earning their own keep in the world.

Own a cheap bike?

It's Actually a GOOD Thing

You need to pedal harder just to go the same distance, helping you get into great shape.

I have a cheap bike. So while I am pedalling hard to keep up, I say to myself, *This is good for you, Jen.*

Break your leg?

It's Actually a GOOD Thing

It makes you realize how wonderful it is just to walk.

I have never broken my leg, but my husband has, and I see how happy he is just to walk again without crutches. I also know that when I have a really tough migraine, and I get those sometimes, it feels so wonderful just to have your head stop pounding. These incidents make me realize how good *normal* feels.

Don't own expensive jewelry?

It's Actually a GOOD Thing

No worries that it's stolen or lost.

I have had some close calls with misplacing expensive jewelry. Now I like to wear fun costume jewelry, which frees me from the stress of loss.

Not a supermodel?

It's Actually a GOOD Thing

You can eat when you're hungry.

I love to eat and can't imagine how much discipline it must take to look that thin.

Lose something and
then find it again?

It's Actually a GOOD Thing

It makes you appreciate it more than before.

I clean my ring and forget to put it back on. It is wrapped in a tissue and could have easily been thrown out. Boy, does that ring look more beautiful than I remember when I find it!

Don't have talent or intelligence or any skills?

It's Actually a GOOD Thing

It's an advantage to becoming a politician.

This job is pretty unfair. It's just that some decisions made by our politicians make you wonder! Nevertheless, as much as we complain about politicians, how many of us are willing to run for office and be the target of public criticism?

Have a broken heart?

It's Actually a GOOD Thing

It helps you lose weight, because you don't feel like eating much. It's also good material if you're a songwriter or aspire to writing a bestselling novel.

Yes, I have had my heart broken and more than once. I lose weight when this happens, because I don't eat much when I'm upset. A friend tells me that it's the opposite for her, so I guess it's possible to gain weight as well. In any case, I did write a bestselling novel called *My Mothers Secret*, and I am also starting to write songs.

Can't find a hotel room, as they are fully booked from an unforeseen emergency?

It's Actually a GOOD Thing

You stay with people who open up their homes and make friends for life.

This actually happens. During 9/11, airplanes were redirected away from the US to Canada. In the Maritime Provinces, there was simply not enough accommodation for all the stranded passengers. Local residents responded by opening their homes for strangers, and lifelong friendships were formed as a result.

Hard of hearing and only
catch parts of conversations?

It's Actually a GOOD Thing

You think people are saying good things about you all the time.

My dad is hard of hearing, so when he asks me what someone just said, I tell him that people are saying nice things about him. Good for everyone.

Not athletic and didn't
make any school teams?

It's Actually a GOOD Thing

You don't have to worry about bad knees or fractured skulls later.

I was not athletic and did not make any school teams, but I also escaped the sports injuries that people complain about later in life.

Living in a cold country?

It's Actually a GOOD Thing

Warm countries have a way to make money from your holidays.

I live in Canada … you know the rest.

Lose power to your house?

It's Actually a GOOD Thing

Your kid can't play computer games for a few hours.

My son does stop playing computer games for a while.

Going on a trip and have really old, scruffy luggage?

It's Actually a GOOD Thing

No one is going to steal from your bags, so your valuables are safe.

I don't have fancy luggage for this reason.

Really mad and send a scouring e-mail but to the wrong address?

It's Actually a GOOD Thing

You cool down and realize
that you could have ruined
a longtime friendship.

Secretary Stanton, angry with an officer who disobeyed an order, said to Abraham Lincoln, "I want to give that man a piece of my mind." Abraham Lincoln replied, "Do so. Make it sharp. Cut him all up." When the secretary asked, "Whom can I send it by?" Abraham Lincoln said. "Why, don't send it at all. Tear it up. You have freed your mind on the subject, and that is all that is necessary. Tear it up. You never want to send such letters. I never do."

I learn from Abraham Lincoln's wisdom and never send e-mails written in anger.

Moving and have to pack?

It's Actually a GOOD Thing

It makes you throw out stuff
you never used anyway, and
you feel so much lighter.

It's hard for me to throw things out when they still fit or work. It's the immigrant upbringing in me. I need a physical move to another house to purge.

Not popular in high school?

It's Actually a GOOD Thing

You end up focusing more
on your studies and then
do better later in life.

By now, you may have guessed that I was not
popular in high school. I did not have a boyfriend,
and I did not go to the prom. However, I did have
all this free time to study, so I attended university
on scholarships earned by achieving high marks.

Weather is cloudy for your outing?

It's Actually a GOOD Thing

You don't have to wear the annoying sunscreen that can clog your pores.

I find sunscreen a nuisance because it makes my skin break out.

Stuck in traffic?

It's Actually a GOOD Thing

Beats being in the accident
that caused the delay.

Traffic is getting worse all the time, so I think about strategies to keep it from bothering me. Sometimes, I recite speeches I am going to be giving. Alone in the car, I can practice without annoying anyone.

Small?

It's Actually a GOOD Thing

Airplane seats are bearable.

I am small, and I still find those airplane seats tough to take, despite the words above.

Live with a teenager?

It's Actually a GOOD Thing

It makes you think it's okay that they go away to school.

I am writing this after I just said good-bye to my son, who is starting university. Like all teenagers, he is breaking away from the child within, and this struggle finds me caught in the middle sometimes. He is ready to go, but I still cry for an hour when I get home.

Accidentally erase an important document?

It's Actually a GOOD Thing

In the rewrite you realize
a major error that would
have been embarrassing.

I have accidentally erased work, and when that happens, abusive language usually follows. Nevertheless, I form a habit of telling myself that perhaps it will be better the second time and that maybe the original was erased for a reason. If I don't think this way, I will be too discouraged to produce better work.

Have a mean boyfriend?

It's Actually a GOOD Thing

It makes you realize that you don't want to marry anyone like that

I never had a mean boyfriend, but I have dated someone mean, and that was enough.

Getting older?

It's Actually a GOOD Thing

You can't stay mad because
you can't remember what
you were mad about.

I have been mad, even when I couldn't remember
why I was mad in the first place. It makes me realize
that it's just not worth staying mad and holding all
that negative energy.

Have to save for everything?

It's Actually a GOOD Thing

It makes you really savor what it is that you can finally afford.

When my husband and I bought our first house after saving to come up with the deposit, we cherished our place. It is a semi-detached house that is seventeen feet wide. There is a two-foot strip of land beside the walkway that we call our front yard. I planted so many flowers on this narrow strip that it looks rather ridiculous, but we love it.

Not getting what you want?

It's Actually a GOOD Thing

It turns out better, and then you realize that you don't always know what you want.

This reminds me of a Garth Brooks song, one of my favorites. The song starts out by describing a high school reunion where he sees the girl of his dreams. The lyrics beautifully describe how much he longed to be with her in high school. You begin to feel sorry for him when unexpectedly, the song does a complete turn. He realizes that he has nothing in common with the girl he thought he wanted, and he is grateful for the girl that he married after all. The song is called "Thank God for Unanswered Prayers."

Can't form a sentence?

It's Actually a GOOD Thing

E-mails today are all point form anyway, and people appreciate communication that is concise.

This comment is just an observation about how people communicate today.

Got fired?

It's Actually a GOOD Thing

Chances are, it wasn't a
good fit, and something
better will show up.

I love the investment business, and I would have
continued along this path if there had not been a
catalyst for change. In many ways, I am grateful
for a chance to see what else I can do.

Not an intellectual?

It's Actually a GOOD Thing

You don't bore people at parties.

This comment is harsh; there must be one or two who are interesting.

Not an expert?

It's Actually a GOOD Thing

It's easier for you to think outside the box.

Sometimes a fresh, unencumbered look can solve the problem better.

Picky eater?

It's Actually a GOOD Thing

Diets are a breeze for you.

You must know someone like this who is thin without trying.

English is not your first language?

It's Actually a GOOD Thing

You're fluent in a language that others are trying to learn.

English is not my first language. We spoke Chinese at home when I was a child. Now, everyone wants to learn Chinese. Who knew!

Not rich?

It's Actually a GOOD Thing

He's not with you for the money.

I didn't have any money when I was married—one less thing to worry about.

Playing poker with a bad hand
that you think is good?

It's Actually a GOOD Thing

People think you're good at bluffing.

When I first learned to play poker, I misunderstood the rules and played with a bad hand that I thought was good. This misinterpretation made people think I was good at bluffing. The truth is, I am horrible at bluffing.

Have backaches?

It's Actually a GOOD Thing

You can be a regular at the spa.

I have chronic back pain. For me, its spa-ah!

Short?

It's Actually a GOOD Thing

Someone yells, "Duck!"
and you're already there.

I'm short and don't worry about hitting my head on low ceilings or lighting fixtures. There are some benefits.

Only had one girlfriend?

It's Actually a GOOD Thing

You're not messed up wondering if you married the right one.

I have seen happiness studies, and contrary to what you may think, research suggests that too much choice actually makes us unhappy. Not knowing whether we made the right decision bothers us.

Can't afford expensive restaurants?

It's Actually a GOOD Thing

It's the same food, but less on the plate and made to look artistic.

I am just as happy with hamburger as I am with steak, so expensive restaurants are wasted on me.

Middle child or didn't get
a lot of attention?

It's Actually a GOOD Thing

It helps you become more independent and less caring about what others think about you.

My mother is one of twelve children. She tells me that her mother would introduce her as *my plain daughter.* My mother evolved into someone who doesn't need a lot of attention to be happy.

Can't ski?

It's Actually a GOOD Thing

You don't have to spend money
on expensive equipment
and clothing to match.

I can ski…but it's not pretty.

Impoverished childhood?

It's Actually a GOOD Thing

You'll work harder to better yourself and end up more successful than the kids who grow up with private jets.

My parents came to Canada with two hundred dollars. I didn't have much growing up, and it was probably the best thing that could have happened to me.

Don't have a nice car?

It's Actually a GOOD Thing

Dents and scratches don't bother you.

Ever been in a car with someone who just got a new car? They are so careful about where they park and any minor scratch is a major issue. Then, after a few years, they'll park anywhere, and the scratches don't seem to matter either.

Had a fight?

It's Actually a GOOD Thing

It makes you feel closer to the other person if you make up and both of you are truly sorry.

I believe that relationships cannot heal unless both sides say sorry and truly feel that way.

Live beside a house that
is so much nicer?

It's Actually a GOOD Thing

The robber is going to your neighbor first.

I heard this comment from Ray Kroc in a speech he gave when I was in business school. I still think it's funny.

Have a messy closet?

It's Actually a GOOD Thing

You find things you never knew you had, and it feels like free stuff.

Ok, I'll come clean...my closet, it's pretty messy.

Not a movie star?

It's Actually a GOOD Thing

A picture of you after a slight weight gain will not appear on the front cover of *People* magazine.

I've always felt that the scrutiny that is placed on public figures is rather harsh.

Having a long-distance relationship?

It's Actually a GOOD Thing

You focus on what's important
because there's no time to argue
about the small stuff when
you seldom get together.

I have had a long-distance relationship and guess what? We never fought. It is only after we lived in the same city that I realized that we didn't agree on everything!

Missing a meal?

It's Actually a GOOD Thing

When you finally get something to eat, it tastes so much better than you remembered.

I love eating when I am really, really hungry because it tastes so good.

Losing your memory?

It's Actually a GOOD Thing

You can see the same movie twice and still be excited about what's going to happen.

This is scary, but I used to be able to recite in minutiae movies that I had seen. Now, I am lucky if I remember the general plot.

Not winning the lottery?

It's Actually a GOOD Thing

Long-lost relatives and people you barely know don't keep calling you.

Studies show that many people who win the lottery end up broke and unhappy; hard to believe but it happens. Jack Whitaker, who won the $315 million Powerball lottery in 2002, is quoted as saying he wished he'd ripped up the ticket. His granddaughter and daughter died from a drug overdose.

Speaking with a British accent?

It's Actually a GOOD Thing

People just assume you're smart.

Whenever we meet with management teams from the UK, I always have to remind myself not to be influenced by the British accent. It makes them sound so clever!

Traveling for business?

It's Actually a GOOD Thing

You don't feel guilty about ordering room service.

I travel for business quite often, and even though I am frugal by nature, I love to order room service and have dinner in my PJs.

Missing home?

It's Actually a GOOD Thing

It just feels so good when you finally sleep in your own bed.

I miss home easily, which is not exactly conducive to being an international fund manager. I still travel extensively.

Down on your luck?

It's Actually a GOOD Thing

You get to know who your
true friends are but you
probably knew this already.

When you're in the investment business, you
understand that there are ups and downs, as
is inevitable with business cycles. Nevertheless,
when I am down, I instinctively know who my true
friends are, and I am very thankful for them.

Hope you have a great day!

If it doesn't go exactly the way you want, could it actually be a good thing?

The thoughts in this book come from my personal life experiences and observations.

In my investment career, I have interviewed managers of numerous international companies. Meeting and getting to know people from around the world helps me realize that we are not all that different.

All of us have dreams, all of us pursue happiness, all of us want to love and be loved. None of us escape disappointment or suffering of one kind or another, and yet, we still get up each morning to do our best for another day.

Isn't that courageous? Isn't that worth celebrating?

I hope you have enjoyed a glimpse of yourself in this book because truly, my experiences are not unique. You and I have both been there.